# President

Julie Murray

Abdo
MY GOVERNMENT
Kids

**abdopublishing.com**

Published by Abdo Kids, a division of ABDO, PO Box 398166, Minneapolis, Minnesota 55439.
Copyright © 2018 by Abdo Consulting Group, Inc. International copyrights reserved in all countries.
No part of this book may be reproduced in any form without written permission from the publisher.

Printed in the United States of America, North Mankato, Minnesota.

102017

012018

 THIS BOOK CONTAINS
RECYCLED MATERIALS

Photo Credits: AP Images, Getty Images, Glow Images, iStock, Shutterstock,
©US Army p.11,22, ©US White House p.15,22

Production Contributors: Teddy Borth, Jennie Forsberg, Grace Hansen

Design Contributors: Christina Doffing, Candice Keimig, Dorothy Toth

Publisher's Cataloging in Publication Data

Names: Murray, Julie, author.

Title: President / by Julie Murray.

Description: Minneapolis, Minnesota : Abdo Kids, 2018. | Series: My government |
    Includes glossary, index and online resource (page 24).

Identifiers: LCCN 2017942866 | ISBN 9781532103995 (lib.bdg.) | ISBN 9781532105111 (ebook) |
    ISBN 9781532105678 (Read-to-me ebook)

Subjects: LCSH: Presidents--United States--Juvenile literature. | United States--History--Juvenile
    literature.

Classification: DDC 352.230973--dc23

LC record available at https://lccn.loc.gov/2017942866

# Table of Contents

# President

Being president is a big job!

Montana
North Dakota
Minnesota
New Hampshire
Vermont
Maine
ho
South Dakota
Wisconsin
Massachusetts
Wyoming
New York
Rhode Island
Michigan
Connecticut
Utah
Nebraska
Iowa
Pennsylvania
New Jersey
Ohio
Delaware
Colorado
Illinois
Indiana
Washington, D.C.
West
Virginia
Maryland
Kansas
Missouri
Virginia
zona
Kentucky
New Mexico
Oklahoma
Tennessee
North Carolina
Arkansas
South
Carolina
Texas
Alabama
Georgia
Mississippi
Louisiana
Florida

Alaska

Hawaii

5

They live in the White House.

They work there too!

They help run the country.

They sign laws.

They command the

US **Armed Forces**.

10

They meet with other leaders. They try to make the world better.

13

They fly on an airplane.

It is called Air Force One.

They had to be born in the USA.

They must be at least 35.

People **vote** for who they want.

It happens every 4 years.

19

Nora meets the president.

# What is the President's Job?

**Commander in Chief**
**(leader of the military)**

**Government Leader**
**(oversee many departments)**

**Head of State**
**(symbol of the country)**

**World Leader**
**(works with other countries)**

# Glossary

**Armed Forces**
a country's military forces, especially its army, navy, and air force.

**vote**
a formal decision one makes (usually on a ballot) between two or more people for a job.

# Index

Visit **abdokids.com** and
use this code to access crafts,
games, videos, and more!

Abdo Kids Code:
## MPK3995